Diet recommendations for TCM - Liver - Qi stagnation

Please check these recommendations always with a TCM nutrition consultant, therapist, doctor or dietician. The recipes and the list of ingredients are supporting also the conventional medical therapy. The calorie disclosures of fresh ingredients (fruit and vegetables) vary according to quality and time of harvest. The contents were checked by a dietician and a nutrition consultant for the Traditional Chinese Medicine (TCM).

Author:
©2017 Josef Miligui
www.ebns.at

AF285287

Source:
The lists are created from the EBNS database for nutritional counseling. The database is used by dietitians, therapists and doctors for advising the patient / client.

Literature:
The specialist literature and the training documents of the German and Austrian dietary and traditional Chinese medicine serve as a knowledge base. We have used the documents as a basis of knowledge, adapted it to our experience and completed them.
http://di-book.com

Title Photo:
©2008 Erika Weixlbaumer

Production and publishing:
BoD – Books on Demand, Norderstedt
ISBN: 9783752861303

Diet recommendations for TCM - Liver - Qi stagnation

1 Treatment strategy

Difficult to solve with food alone, spread liver QI, move.
Hot - NO, cold - NO, sour - LITTLE, everything else YES, especially BITTER

2 Avoid

Too fat, late at night, red meat, spicy hot spices, too much garlic and onion, alcohol, ready meals, denatured food, emotional pressure, stress, perfectionism, lack of exercise, physical stiffness.

3 Breakfast

4 Snack

5 Lunch

6 Afternoon

7 Dinner

8   Any time

9 Recipes

(recommendable) = You can use more.
(little) = You should use less than specified or omit.

9.1 8 treasures of rice

Strengthens kidney and bladder, builds up Qi, strengthens the spleen, repels moisture, reduces internal heat, prevents cancer, builds heart, calms nerves.
Cooking time approx. 1 hour
Calories p. portion: 212
4 portions

Quantity of ingredients:
Lily bulbs 1 table spoon / 5g. (recommended)................................. *
Longane 1 table spoon / 5g. (yes) .... *
King Solomon's-seal 1 table spoon / 5g. (recommended)................. *
Yam root, yam root tuber 1 table spoon / 5g. (recommended)........... *
Coix (seeds) YiYi Ren 1 table spoon / 5g. (yes)............................... *
Rice wild (nature rice) 1 1/2 cups / 240g. (yes) .... metal
Water 8-10 cups / 800g. (yes) .... earth

Cooking instructions:
Each one 1 tbsp: Bai He, Longan, Yu Zhu, Da Zao, Shan Yao, Lian Mi, Yi Yi Ren, Qian Shi
Add hot water and soak for about 30 minutes. Then add 1 - 2 cups of rice (normal) and simmer for 1/2 to 1 hour until the rice is very soft. Or: Cook for about 3 hours with the herbs a congee. Then the herbs do not have to be soaked.

9.2 Adzuki Bean and Rice Soup

Reduces moisture, directs down, reduces gastrointestinal heat, builds up essence, strengthens muscles after heat illness, builds up fluids.
Cooking time approx. 2 hours
Calories p. portion: 199
1 portions

Quantity of ingredients:
Adzuki beans 8 table spoons / 40g. (recommended)................. water
Rice round grain 2 table spoons / 20g. (recommended)............. metal
Water 1 1/2 cups / 200g. (yes)... earth
Honey 1 table spoon / 8g. () .... earth

Cooking instructions:
Boil soaked adzuki beans and round grain rice in a ratio of 4: 1 in water until a thin pulp has formed. Sweet as needed; possibly puree.

Effect: This recipe strengthens kidney, spleen and stomach and is particularly suitable for mothers with too little milk flow.

9.3 Apple sauce with raisins

Nourishes fluids, reduces stomach heat, strengthens spleen, harmonizes stomach, moisturizes, relaxes, builds up Qi.
Cooking time approx. 25 min
Calories p. portion: 74
10 portions
Allergens: O

Quantity of ingredients:
Apple (sweet) 2,2 lbs / 1000g. (recommended).......................... earth
Water 1/2 cup / 100g. (yes)... earth
Raisins 1/8 lbs - 2oz / 50g. (yes)... earth

Cooking instructions:
Wash, peel and quarter the apples and remove the core. Put the apples with the water in a pot. Wash the raisins with hot water and add them. Cook at low heat for about 10 minutes, then allow to cool. For children up to 10 months, mash in the blender finely. For the larger ones, crush with the potato steamer. Fill and seal in a freezer or empty yoghurt jug. Close the yoghurt jug. Freeze in the shock freezer.
If necessary, thaw at room temperature for about 6 hours. (Lasting about 4 months).
The fruit mousse is intended as dessert or intermediate meal. It has an anti-digestive effect. In case of diarrhea give better banana.

9.4 Barley mash with berries

Forces essence, forces spleen, cools bladder, diuretic, relaxes, builds up Qi, spreads, moisturises dryness.
Cooking time approx. 2 hours
Calories p. portion: 113
5 portions
Allergens: A

Quantity of ingredients:

Water 10 cups / 1200g. (yes)... earth
Barley 1 cup / 120g. (recommended).. earth
Ginger fresh 2 slices / 2g. (little) ....metal
Cardamom 3 capsules / 1g. (recommended) ....*
Salt 1 pinch / 1g. (recommended)..water
Raspberry 5/8 lbs - 8oz / 250g. (little) ....wood
Cocoa 1 pinch / 1g. (little).. fire
Barley malt 1 table spoon / 15g. (recommended)...................... earth
Lemon Balm (fresh) 2-4 leaves / 3g. (recommended) ....metal

Cooking instructions:

Boil the barley with water, ginger and cardamom pods in a large saucepan. Close pot with a lid and cook over low heat for about 2 hours.

For 2 servings of cooked barley porridge, place about 2 ladles in a bowl. Stir with sunflower seeds, malt, cocoa powder and a pinch of salt. Stir fresh berries into the porridge and serve sprinkled with fresh mint or lemon balm.

Tip: The pre-cooked barley porridge (without fruit) can be stored well in the refrigerator and used for sweet or savory dishes, e.g. with stewed vegetables or fruit seasoned compote.

9.5   Barley soup

Works neutral to slightly warming and relaxes the Qi flow. Helps with loss of appetite and diarrhea due to spleen weakness. With weak spleen qi, one should often eat salty soups for breakfast.
Cooking time approx. 25 min
Calories p. portion: 265
2 portions
Allergens: A

Quantity of ingredients:

Barley 1 cup / 120g. (recommended).. earth
Salt 1 pinch / 1g. (recommended)..water
Ginger fresh 1/2 teaspoon / 1g. (little).......................................metal
Olive oil 1 table spoon / 10g. (recommended)........................... earth
Parsley 2 table spoons / 30g. (little)..wood
Water 1 1/2 cups / 240g. (yes)... earth

Cooking instructions:
Roast the barley in the pan, then grind it to the ground, and boil with water, some salt and ginger to a mash. Before serving add oil and parsley.

Variant: You can add a better taste to the dish if you cook it with prepared vegetable or meat broth.

9.6   Basic recipe for a chicken broth worming

Strengthens Qi and blood, is very warm.
Cooking time approx. 2-3 hours
Calories p. portion: 90
9 portions
Allergens: L

Quantity of ingredients:
Chicken meat 1/2 piece / 600g. (recommended)......................wood
Carrot 2 pieces / 150g. (recommended)................................... earth
Leek 1 stick / 45g. (little)..metal
Celery root 1 piece / 500g. (recommended)............................. earth
Ginger fresh 2 slices / 2g. (little) ....metal
Fenugreek 1 teaspoon / 2g. (recommended) ....*
Juniper berry 1 teaspoon / 3g. (little).. fire
Bay leaf 3 pieces / 2g. (recommended) ....*
Water 4 cup / 900g. (yes).. earth

Cooking instructions:
Remove chicken parts from fat. Place chicken pieces in a saucepan with hot water and heat till it boils briefly, skimming any resulting foam. Add coarsely chopped vegetables and all spices and cook over medium heat for 2 to 3 hours. Strain the finished soup. Throw away vegetables and bones.
Tip: If you want to use the meat as a soup insert, take out after 45 minutes and return only the bones in the soup.
Refrigerate for later use.

9.7 Basic recipe for a reissue soup (Congee)

Warms the stomach and spleen, harmonizes the intestine, forces Qi, reduces moisture.
Cooking time approx. 2-4 hours
Calories p. portion: 140
3 portions

Quantity of ingredients:
Rice variety any 1 cup / 120g. (recommended)..........................metal
Water 6 cups / 700g. (yes) .... earth

Cooking instructions:
Cook rice and water in a ratio of about 1: 6. The amount of water determines the thickness of the mash (matter of taste).
Put the rice in a saucepan with a heavy lid. It is important to simmer the rice after a short boil on the slightest flame, otherwise it burns.
Boil the rice for 2-4 hours. The longer he cooks, the more he strengthens.
If you want to eat the dish for breakfast, you can put the rice on just before bedtime.
To be on the safe side, you should first check the behavior of your pot and cooker under observation for a similar amount of time, so that nothing burns.
Refrigerate for later use.

9.8 Beef broth

Warming and nourishing, builds up Qi, strengthens blood and fluids.
Cooking time approx. 2-6 hours
Calories p. portion: 125
7 portions
Allergens: L

Quantity of ingredients:
Water 4 cup / 1000g. (yes) .... earth
Lemon 2 dashes / 2g. () ....wood
Beef meat 1,1 lbs / 500g. (yes)... earth
Beef meatbones 2 pieces / 0g. (yes).. earth
Turmeric (yellow root) 1 pinch / 1g. (recommended) ....*
Carrot 2 pieces / 100g. (recommended).................................... earth
Celery root 1 inch / 25g. (recommended)................................... earth
Parsley root 1 piece / 150g. (recommended) .... earth
Onion white 1 piece / 50g. (little)..metal

Bay leaf 2-3 leaves / 2g. (recommended) ....*
Coriander 1/2 teaspoon / 2g. (recommended)...........................metal
Ginger fresh 1 inch / 2g. (little)..metal
Wakame 1 inch / 1g. (recommended)......................................water
Parsley 1 stem / 10g. (little)..wood

Cooking instructions:
In a saucepan with water (enough to cover the meat), add a few drops
of lemon juice, a little turmeric, beef and bones, heat till it boils and
simmer for a while; then pour away the whole broth, clean the pot, rinse
off meat and bones with hot water (this will save you from foaming) and
put it back to the saucepan with hot water (amount as you like); add a
good pinch of turmeric, carrot, celery, parsley root to the pot; add onion,
bay leaves, coriander, a piece of sliced ginger, a strip of wakame, a
stalk of parsley; boil everything together and simmer for 2-6 hours (if the
meat is to be used otherwise, take it out of the broth after 1 1/2 - 2
hours, as soon as it is cooked, the bones are returned to the broth);
When the cooking time is over, pour the broth through a sieve and
discard all ingredients.

Notes: The longer the broth has cooked, the warmer but more
nourishing it is. It is after cooling for 3-4 days in the refrigerator durable.
The broth can be drunk hot or used as a base for soups with cereals,
potatoes and fresh vegetables.

9.9   Broccoli cream soup

Nourishes lung Yin, produces humors, strengthens spleen and liver,
moisturizes, reduces cold-evil, softens knots.
Cooking time approx. 30 min
Calories p. portion: 98
6 portions
Allergens: LO

Quantity of ingredients:
Olive oil 2 table spoons / 7g. (recommended) .... earth
Broccoli 1,1 lbs / 500g. (recommended)................................... earth
Carrot 2 pieces / 150g. (recommended)................................... earth
Potato 2 pieces / 120g. (yes).. earth
Onion white 1 piece / 50g. (little)...metal
Water 1 cup / 50g. (yes).. earth
Basic recipe for a vegetable soup 2 cup / 500g. (recommended) ....*
White wine 1/2 cup / 125g. (little)...wood

Sage 1 teaspoon / 2g. (yes) .... fire
Rosemary 1 teaspoon / 2g. (little) .... fire
Pepper (ground) 1 pinch / 0,5g. (recommended) .... metal
Salt 1 pinch / 1g. (recommended) .... water

Cooking instructions:
Add the olive oil to the pan, add the washed and cut broccoli, diced carrots and potatoes, sauté for a short time, add the chopped onion, fill with water, enough water to cover the vegetables at least 3 finger breadths. Add bouillon, salt, add a little bit of white wine, add the seasoned sage and rosemary.
Heat till it boils and then simmer on a small fire for about 25 minutes.
Season with pepper, if necessary season with sea salt. Purée the soup.

9.10 Carrot and rice gruel soup

Warms the stomach and spleen, harmonizes the intestine, forces Qi, reduces moisture, strengthens spleen and liver, regulates Qi flow, moisturizes, relaxes, builds up Qi, spreads.
Cooking time approx. 10 min
Calories p. portion: 101
1 portions

Quantity of ingredients:
Basic recipe for a rice soup (Congee) 1 cup / 120g. (yes) .... *
Carrot 2 pieces / 100g. (recommended) .... earth
Salt 1 teaspoon / 4g. (recommended) .... water

Cooking instructions:
Peel and grate carrots. Heat the rice soup (according to the basic recipe) till it boils and add the grated carrots and salt. Cook for 10 minutes.

9.11 Celery juice

Strengthens stomach Qi, moisturizes, relaxes, builds up Qi, spreads.
Cooking time approx. 5 min
Calories p. portion: 33
1 portions
Allergens: L

Quantity of ingredients:
Celery root 1/2 piece / 200g. (recommended)........................... earth
Water 1 cup / 120g. (yes)... earth
Salt 1 pinch / 0,5g. (recommended)...water

Cooking instructions:
Peel celeriac and cut into pieces and juice. Mix with water and salt as needed.

9.12 Cooling rice dish with grapefruit

Lowers lung Qi, nourishes fluids, dissolves mucus, dries out, passes downwardly, warms the stomach and spleen, harmonizes the intestine, forces Qi, reduces moisture, strengthens Qi and Kidney Jing, moisturizes, relaxes, builds up Qi, spreads.
Cooking time approx. 20 min
Calories p. portion: 234
4 portions
Allergens: GHO

Quantity of ingredients:
Rice round grain 1 cup / 120g. (recommended) ....metal
Water 5 cups / 600g. (yes) .... earth
Hazelnuts 2 table spoons / 20g. (recommended)...................... earth
Raisins 2 table spoons / 20g. (yes).. earth
Agave nectar 1 table spoon / 10g. (recommended)...........................*
Salt 1 pinch / 0,2g. (recommended)..water
Almond puree 1 table spoon / 10g. (yes) .... earth
Grapefruit (Pomelo) 1 piece / 200g. (recommended) .... fire
Butter organic 2 teaspoons / 20g. (recommended) .... earth

Cooking instructions:
Preparation on the eve: Pour round grain rice into cold water and cook. Soak chopped hazelnuts and raisins in some hot water overnight.

In the morning: Stir in a little hot water some agave syrup; add the rice and heat; add a small pinch of salt, almond paste, chopped grapefruit, the soaked chopped hazelnuts and raisins and mix; Serve with a small piece of butter.

9.13 Grape compote

Moisturizes, relaxes, builds up Qi, spreads, moisten the lungs and large intestine.
Cooking time approx. 10 min
Calories p. portion: 128
1 portions
Allergens: H

Quantity of ingredients:
Grapes red 3/8 lbs - 6oz / 150g. (recommended)...................... earth
Water 4 table spoons / 30g. (yes).. earth
Almond 1 teaspoon / 3g. (recommended).................................. earth

Cooking instructions:
Remove the grapes from the stems, wash thoroughly in warm water and drain. Halve the grapes (remove the seeds for babies). In a small saucepan, heat 4 tablespoons of water with the grapes and the grated almonds till it boils . Cook over low heat for about 3 minutes, then chill. (For babies lukewarm).

9.14 Grapefruit juice

Nourishes fluids, passes downwardly, forms body fluid.
Cooking time approx. 5 min
Calories p. portion: 107
1 portions

Quantity of ingredients:
Grapefruit (Pomelo) 1 cup / 250g. (recommended) .... fire

Cooking instructions:
Juice fresh grapefruit or use organic juice.

9.15 Lentils and rice stew

Strengthens spleen and liver, regulates Qi flow, moisturizes, relaxes, builds up Qi, spreads, warms the stomach and spleen, harmonizes the intestine, forces Qi, reduces moisture, brings the liver Qi in motion, cools heat.
Cooking time approx. 25 min
Calories p. portion: 232
3 portions
Allergens: LNO

Quantity of ingredients:
Lentils 1/4 lbs - 4oz / 100g. (little) .... water
Water 5 cups / 500g. (yes) .... earth
Rice variety any 1 cup / 120g. (recommended) .... metal
Sesame oil 1 table spoon / 10g. (recommended) .... earth
Carrot 2 pieces / 150g. (recommended) .... earth
Celery sticks 2 rods / 20g. (recommended) .... earth
Cumin (Caraway seed) 1 pinch / 0,2g. (recommended) .... metal
Salt 1 pinch / 0,5g. (recommended) .... water
Vinegar (Apple vinegar) 1 dash / 2g. (little) .... wood
Parsley 2 table spoons / 18g. (little) .... wood

Cooking instructions:
Soak the dry lentils the day before.
Heat sesame oil in a hot pot; cut carrot and celery into small pieces and
sauté; add rice, a pinch of cumin and lentils and heat till it boils.
If the lenses are soft, add salt; season with a little vinegar and garnish
with parsley.

Variant: In summer you can omit the cumin and add fresh green peas,
Chinese cabbage or celery.

9.16 Pumpkin soup

Forces lungs and spleen, diuretic, forces Qi, protects liver, forces Qi,
forces spleen, relieves inflammation, moisturizes, relaxes, builds up Qi,
spreads, strengthens spleen and liver, regulates Qi flow, moisturizes,
relaxes, builds up Qi, spreads.
Cooking time approx. 1 hour
Calories p. portion: 105
3 portions

Quantity of ingredients:
Pumpkin 3/4 lbs / 300g. (yes) .... earth
Carrot 2 pieces / 100g. (recommended) .... earth
Potato 2 pieces / 120g. (yes) .... earth
Olive oil 1 table spoon / 10g. (recommended) .... earth
Onion white 1 piece / 50g. (little) .... metal
Water 1 cup / 120g. (yes) .... earth
Parsley 1 table spoon / 7g. (little) .... wood
Anise (Common Fennel) 1 pinch / 1g. (little) .... earth
Salt 1 pinch / 1g. (recommended) .... water

Cooking instructions:
Add the olive oil to the pan, add the diced pumpkin, diced carrots and potatoes. Roast them shortly, add the finely chopped onion, fill with water, add enough water to cover the vegetables at least 3 finger-widths. Boil at low heat.

Season with sea salt, add small cutted parsley, a pinch of anise (little). Allow to simmer for about 35 minutes. Then purée the soup and add some water, depending on the consistency of the soup.

9.17 Reissue soup with seaweed

Forces Qi and blood, reduces cold, forces spleen, liver and stomach, strengthens blood and Qi, regulates Qi, warms spleen and kidney, dissolves stagnation, directs upwards.
Cooking time approx. 4-5 hours
Calories p. portion: 130
6 portions
Allergens: L

Quantity of ingredients:
Beef meatbones 3/4 lbs / 10g. (yes) .... earth
Beef soup meat 7/8 lbs / 400g. (recommended) .... earth
Parsley 1/4 Bunch / 25g. (little) .... wood
Juniper berry 4 / 2g. (little) .... fire
Carrot 2 pieces / 180g. (recommended) .... earth
Celery root 1/4 lbs / 100g. (recommended) .... earth
Onion (spring onion) 1/2 piece / 10g. (little) .... metal
Peppercorns 4 / 1g. (little) .... metal
Lovage 1 Twig / 3g. (recommended) .... metal
Wakame 1 inch / 3g. (recommended) .... water
Rice variety any 2 table spoons / 20g. (recommended) .... metal
Water 4 cup / 900g. (yes) .... earth

Cooking instructions:
Boil parsley in water. Add the juniper berries, meat bones, a piece of soup, carrot and a piece of celery tuber, a separately tanned onion half, a few peppery grains, a belly and a piece of wakame algae; Allow 4-8 hours to simmer and then strain. Add the rice and simmer for another 1/2 hour. Keep the stock in the refrigerator.
Variant: If you remove the meat after 1-2 hours, you can still dice it well and use it later as a supporter.

9.18 Rice congee with carrots and fennel

Nutritious builds up Qi, forces the digestive functions.
Cooking time approx. 2 hours and more
Calories p. portion: 131
3 portions
Allergens: G

Quantity of ingredients:
Basic recipe for a rice soup (Congee) 2 cup / 500g. (yes) .... *
Carrot 2 pieces / 100g. (recommended) .... earth
Fennel 1 piece / 250g. (little) .... earth
Butter organic 1 teaspoon / 3g. (recommended) .... earth
Cardamom 1/2 teaspoon / 1g. (recommended) .... *

Cooking instructions:
Cook rice congee according to basic recipe.
Clean and cut carrots and fennel.

When carrots and fennel are cooked from the beginning, they serve wholesomeness. If added shortly before the end of the cooking time, taste and vitamins are retained.

Refine with butter and cardamom before serving.

9.19 Rice noodle soup with shiitake mushrooms

Strengthens spleen and liver, regulates Qi flow, relaxes, builds up Qi, spreads, dries out, passes downwardly, strengthens stomach Qi, nourishes Yin of the lungs, stomach and colon, supports digestion, reduces internal wind.
Cooking time approx. 20 min
Calories p. portion: 66
2 portions
Allergens: L

Quantity of ingredients:
Rice noodles 2 handful / 20g. (yes) ....metal
Shiitake, dried 4-6 pieces / 5g. (recommended) .... earth
Basic recipe for a vegetable soup (nutritious) 1 1/2 cups / 240g.
(recommended)*
Chinese cabbage 1 cup / 60g. (recommended) .... earth
Lovage 1 teaspoon / 3g. (recommended) ....metal
Miso 2 table spoons / 18g. (recommended) ....water

Cooking instructions:
Soak rice noodles and shiitake mushrooms separately in cold water. Heat the vegetable broth and add the soaked shiitake mushrooms cut into strips and simmer gently. Cut Chinese cabbage into noodles, add lovage green and rice noodles and let it steep for a while. Before serving, stir in Miso dissolved in a little cooled water. Recommendation: Suitable at the beginning of each meal, also for breakfast

9.20 Rice porridge with orange peel

Warms the stomach and spleen, harmonizes the intestine, forces Qi, reduces moisture. brings the Liver Qi in motion, cools heat, moisturizes, relaxes, builds up Qi, spreads. nourishes blood, moisturizes, relaxes, builds up Qi, spreads.
Cooking time approx. 10 min
Calories p. portion: 120
4 portions
Allergens: L

Quantity of ingredients:
Rice variety any 1 cup / 100g. (recommended)..........................metal
Water 6 cups / 600g. (yes) .... earth
Orange grated peel 1/4 piece / 3g. (recommended)..........................*
Olive oil 1 table spoon / 10g. (recommended)............................ earth
Champignon 1/2 cup / 50g. (recommended)............................... earth
Celery sticks 1/2 bunch / 60g. (recommended) .... earth
Basic recipe for a chicken soup (warming) 3-4 table spoons / 40g. ..*
Salt 1 pinch / 0,5g. (recommended)..water

Cooking instructions:
The day before boil the rice with the orange peel and water in a ratio of about 1: 6. The amount of water determines the thickness of the mash (pure matter of taste). Put the rice in a saucepan with good insulation and a heavy lid. It is important to simmer the rice after a short boil on the slightest flame, otherwise it burns. Boil the rice for 2-4 hours. The longer he cooks, the more he strengthens.
Heat the oil in a saucepan, add the chopped champignon and celery and sauté briefly. Add the rice. Add vegetable broth or water, warm up, salt.

9.21 Rice porridge with shrubs (seeds) Yi Yi Ren

Warms stomach, harmonizes the intestine, forces Qi, reduces moisture, forces spleen, nourishes and forces Lunge, reduces internal heat, moves Qi and blood, diuretic, cools in internal heat.
Cooking time approx. 25 min
Calories p. portion: 212
2 portions

Quantity of ingredients:
Water 4 cups / 450g. (yes) .... earth
Rice variety any 1 cup / 120g. (recommended).........................metal
Lemon peel 1/4 piece / 2g. (yes).. fire
Coix (seeds) YiYi Ren 1/2 cup / 50g. (yes) ....*
Cress 1 table spoon / 6g. (recommended)..............................metal

Cooking instructions:
Cook rice porridge according to basic recipe with a half cup of Yi Yi Ren and lemon peel. Simmer for 1 hour and then sprinkle cress over it.

9.22 Rice with stewed vegetables

Dissipates heat and moisture.
Cooking time approx. 20 min
Calories p. portion: 166
2 portions
Allergens: L

Quantity of ingredients:
Rice variety any 1/2 cup / 60g. (recommended).......................metal
Water 3 cups / 300g. (yes) .... earth
Lemon peel 1 piece / 3g. (yes) .... fire
Water 1/2 cup / 0g. (yes).. earth
Carrot 2 pieces / 180g. (recommended).................................... earth
Celery sticks 1/2 piece / 5g. (recommended) .... earth
Champignon 1/2 cup / 50g. (recommended)............................. earth
Cress 2 table spoons / 20g. (recommended) ....metal
Linseed oil 1 dash / 3g. (recommended).................................. earth

Cooking instructions:
Cook rice according to basic recipe with a piece of lemon peel.
Steam chopped carrots, celery and mushrooms until soft.
Then sprinkle with cress. Then add a dash of high quality cold oil.

9.23 Roasted millet with Celery sticks

Strengthens spleen and kidney, diuretic, brings the liver Qi in motion, cools heat, moisturizes, relaxes, builds up Qi, spreads.
Cooking time approx. 30 min
Calories p. portion: 400
2 portions
Allergens: L

Quantity of ingredients:
Millet 1 cup / 120g. (recommended)... earth
Water 1 1/2 cups / 240g. (yes).. earth
Celery sticks 2 rods / 50g. (recommended)............................... earth
Water 2 table spoons / 30g. (yes).. earth
Herbs various 1 table spoon / 10g. (recommended).........................*
Salt 1 pinch / 1g. (recommended)...water
Sage 3-4 leaves / 2g. (yes)... fire
Cress 1 teaspoon / 3g. (recommended)....................................metal

Cooking instructions:
Roast millet briefly, pour over water, heat till it boils and let stand for 20 min. to swell.

Cut celery into small pieces and mix with water, salt and fresh herbs and cook for 10 min. Add to the millet. Sprinkle fresh sage or watercress over it.

9.24 Roasted nuts

Strengthens kidney Qi, essence and brain, forces kidney, builds up essence, warms lungs, moistens the intestine, moisturizes, relaxes, builds up Qi, spreads.
Cooking time approx. 5 min
Calories p. portion: 973
2 portions
Allergens: H

Quantity of ingredients:
Hazelnuts 1/4 lbs - 4oz / 100g. (recommended)......................... earth
Cashews 1/4 lbs - 4oz / 100g. (recommended).......................... earth
Walnuts 1/4 lbs - 4oz / 100g. (yes) .... earth

Cooking instructions:
Roast nuts in a pan for about 5 minutes.

9.25 Tea from celery sticks

Brings the Liver Qi in motion, cools heat, moisturizes, relaxes, builds up Qi, spreads.
Cooking time approx. 15 min
Calories p. portion: 1
4 portions
Allergens: L

Quantity of ingredients:
Celery sticks 2 table spoons (chopped) / 18g. (recommended).. earth
Water 2 cup / 500g. (yes) .... earth

Cooking instructions:
Heat the water till it boils and put it aside. Add cutted celery and cook for 10 min. to let go. Strain. Sweet to taste with honey.

9.26 Tea from coriander

Sudorific, reduces wind.
Cooking time approx. 10 min
Calories p. portion: 2
4 portions

Quantity of ingredients:
Coriander 1 teaspoon / 3g. (recommended)..............................metal
Water 2 cup / 500g. (yes) .... earth

Cooking instructions:
Heat the water till it boils and put it aside. Add coriander and 10 min. to let go. Sweet to taste with honey. Strain when pouring.

9.27 Tea from ground

Reduces mucus and moist heat in the liver and gallbladder, against liver Qi stagnation, spleen qi deficiency, spleen and kidney Yang- deficit.
Cooking time approx. 10 min
Calories p. portion: 2
4 portions

Quantity of ingredients:
Ground 1 teaspoon / 3g. (recommended) .... earth
Water 2 cup / 500g. (yes) .... earth

Cooking instructions:
Heat the water till it boils and put it aside. Add crushed cumin and leave for 10 min. to let go. Sweet to taste with honey. Strain when pouring.

Drink 1 cup 2 times a day.

9.28 Tea from jasmine blossoms

Forces liver-Qi.
Cooking time approx. 10 min
Calories p. portion: 0
2 portions

Quantity of ingredients:
Jasmine blossoms tee 2 teaspoons / 4g. (recommended)................*
Water 2 cup / 500g. (yes) .... earth

Cooking instructions:
Heat the water till it boils and put it aside. Add jasmine flowers and 10 min. to let go. Sweet to taste with honey. Strain when pouring.

9.29 Tea from lime blossom

Reduces wind-heat and wind-coldness of the lungs.
Cooking time approx. 10 min
Calories p. portion: 0
2 portions

Quantity of ingredients:
Lime blossom tea 1 teabag / 2g. (recommended) ....*
Water 2 cup / 500g. (yes) .... earth

Cooking instructions:
Heat the water till it boils and put it aside. Add the linden blossoms and leave for 10 min. to let go. Sweet to taste with honey. Strain when pouring.

9.30 Tea from marjoram

Dissolves stagnation, directs upwards.
Cooking time approx. 10 min
Calories p. portion: 0
4 portions

Quantity of ingredients:
Marjoram 2 teaspoons / 6g. (recommended) ....metal
Water 2 cup / 500g. (yes).. earth

Cooking instructions:
Heat the water till it boils and put it aside. Add marjoram and 10 min. to
let go. Sweet to taste with honey. Strain when pouring.

9.31 Tea from Melissa

Preserves the fluids, contracts, soothes liver fire, stimulates lungs Qi.
Cooking time approx. 10 min
Calories p. portion: 0
4 portions

Quantity of ingredients:
Balm 2 teaspoons / 4g. (recommended) ....wood
Water 2 cup / 500g. (yes).. earth

Cooking instructions:
Heat the water till it boils and put it aside. Add lemon balm and 10 min.
to let go. Sweet to taste with honey. Strain when pouring.

9.32 Tea from orange blossom

Forces liver - Qi
Cooking time approx. 15 min
Calories p. portion: 0
4 portions

Quantity of ingredients:
Orange blossom 2-4 teaspoons / 6g. (recommended) ....*
Water 2 cup / 500g. (yes).. earth

Cooking instructions:
Heat the water till it boils and put it aside. Add orange blossom and 10
min. to let go. Strain. Sweet to taste with honey.

Drink 1 cup freshly prepared orange blossom tea 3 times a day.

9.33 Tea from passion blossoms

Forces liver-Qi.
Cooking time approx. 10 min
Calories p. portion: 0
4 portions

Quantity of ingredients:
Passion blossoms tea 2-4 teaspoons / 6g. (recommended) ....*
Water 2 cup / 500g. (yes).. earth

Cooking instructions:
Heat the water till it boils and put it aside. Add passion flower tea and let
it rest for 10 min. to let go. Strain. Sweet to taste with honey.

9.34 Tea from rose blossom

Forces liver-Qi.
Cooking time approx. 15 min
Calories p. portion: 0
4 portions

Quantity of ingredients:
Rose blossom tea 2-4 teaspoons / 6g. (recommended) ....*
Water 2 cup / 500g. (yes).. earth

Cooking instructions:
Heat the water till it boils and put it aside. Add rose petals and 10 min.
to let go. Strain. Sweet to taste with honey.

9.35 Thick pea soup

Nourishes Qi, diuretic, harmonizes Qi (especially in the Middle and
Lower), strengthens the kidney and the defense Qi, dischars moisture.
Cooking time approx. 2-3 hours
Calories p. portion: 123
3 portions
Allergens: AN

Quantity of ingredients:
Peas, green 3/8 lbs - 6oz / 150g. (recommended) .... water
Water 2 1/4 cups / 550g. (yes) .... earth
Sesame oil 1 table spoon / 20g. (recommended) .... earth
Onion white 1/2 piece / 25g. (little) .... metal
Ginger fresh 1/2 teaspoon / 1g. (little) .... metal
Ground 1/2 teaspoon / 1g. (recommended) .... earth
Oat meal 1 table spoon / 15g. (little) .... metal
Salt 1 pinch / 1g. (recommended) .... water
Parsley 1 stem / 2g. (little) .... wood

Cooking instructions:
Soak dried peas before cooking. Sauté sesame oil, onion, a little
oatmeal, ginger and cumin in a hot pot; add the peas and simmer for 2-
3 hours; add salt at the end and pruée with a blender; garnish with
parsley.

9.36 Tsampa

Reduces internal heat, dissolves mucus, detoxifies.
Cooking time approx. 5 min
Calories p. portion: 140
2 portions
Allergens: A

Quantity of ingredients:
Tsampa (roasted barley flour) 4 table spoons / 30g. (reco.) .... earth
Green tea 1 cup / 120g. (yes) .... fire
Water 1 cup / 120g. (yes) .... earth

Cooking instructions:
Tsampa is traditionally made with tea.
The tsampa is poured into a bowl and doused with tea, part of which is
drunk and the remainder made into a dough-like mass with tsampa.
You can also pour the tea first; In any case, it takes some skill to
achieve the right balance of tsampa and liquid. The two substances are
usually mixed with your fingers. It is recommended to add yak butter to
improve taste and stability.

9.37 Tsampa with jam or fruit compote

Nourishes fluids, reduces stomach heat, forces spleen, produces essence, harmonizes stomach, moisturizes intestines.
Cooking time approx. 5 min
Calories p. portion: 280
1 portions
Allergens: AGO

Quantity of ingredients:
Tsampa (roasted barley flour) 2 table spoons / 30g. (reco.) .... earth
Water 6-8 table spoons / 70g. (yes).. earth
Butter organic 1/2 teaspoon / 2g. (recommended) .... earth
Strawberry jam 1 table spoon / 7g. (recommended)................... wood
Sunflower seeds 2 teaspoons / 14g. (recommended) .... earth
Apple (sweet) 1 piece grated / 120g. (recommended)................ earth

Cooking instructions:
Pour tsampa with boiling water and stir with a spoon until a porridge is formed.
Add butter, jam, sunflower seeds and grated apple.
Sweet to taste with honey, whole cane sugar, or barley malt.
Spices and herbs: fresh mint, vanilla or cocoa, anise, cinnamon

Summer: jam or compote of your choice
Winter: nuts and apple or pear

9.38 Vegetable miso soup with tofu

Strengthens spleen and liver, regulates Qi flow, moisturizes, relaxes, builds up Qi, spreads, forces Qi, forces liver and kidney, reduces damp heat, detoxifies, nourishes fluids, reduces internal heat, dries out, passes downwardly.
Cooking time approx. 15 min
Calories p. portion: 107
4 portions
Allergens: EN

Quantity of ingredients:
Sesame oil 2 table spoons / 35g. (recommended) .... earth
Onion (shallot) 1 piece / 20g. (little) .... metal
Carrot 1 piece / 70g. (recommended) .... earth
Leek 2 inches / 10g. (little).. metal
Water 3 cups / 750g. (yes) .... earth

Endive salad 2 table spoons / 30g. (yes) .... fire
Soy Tofu 2 table spoons / 30g. (recommended)........................ earth
Ginger fresh 1/2 teaspoon / 1g. (little)....................................metal
Miso 2 table spoons / 15g. (recommended) ....water

Cooking instructions:
In sesame oil first sauté onions, then carrots and a little leek; Pour in water and simmer gently; add the bean sprouts and endive leaves and leave to stand; Tofu cubes, add a little ginger; at the end stir in a little cooled cooking-water the Miso.

10 Effects of food

10.1 Use ingredients: recommendable

Acai powder
Acerola fruit nectar or powder
Adzuki beans
Agave nectar
Agrimony
Almond
Aloe juice
Amaranth Pops
Angelica root
Apple (sweet)
Apple juice (natural cloudy)
Apple puree
Apricot dried
Apricot jam
Apricot nectar
Apricots juice
Arrowroot
Artichoke
Baking powder
Balm
Bamboo shoots
Banchatee (green tea)
barberry
Barley
Barley flour
Barley grass powder
Barley grouts
Barley malt
Barley not peeled
Basic recipe for a beef soup
Basic recipe for a beef soup (warming)
Basic recipe for a chicken soup (warming)
Basic recipe for a duck soup
Basic recipe for a fish soup
Basic recipe for a vegetable soup (nutritious)
Basil
Basil (fresh)
Batavia
Bay leaf
Beans (green, fresh)
Bearberry leaf
Beef bone marrow
Beef heart
Beef heart (calf)
Beef kidney
Beef liver
Beef lungs (calf)

Beef meat (calf)
Beef Oxtail pieces
Beef soup meat
Beer (alcohol-free)
Beer (alcohol-reduced)
Berries of the season
Berry juice
Bitter Herb liqueur
Bitter Lemon
Bitter liqueur
Bitter orange peel
Black beans
Black caraway
Black fungus mushroom
Blackberry dried (unripe fruit)
Blackberry jam
Blackberry leaves
Blackthorn (Sloe)
Blue mallow tee
Blueberry dried
Blueberry jam
Bocksdorn fruits (Fructus Lycii, Goji, goji berry dried
Boletus mushroom
Borage
Borage oil
Brazil nuts
Bread roll
Bread with carob kernel flour
Breadcrumbs (wheat bread, bread roll)
Brie cheese
Broad beans (thick beans)
Broccoli
Brown ale
Brussels sprouts
Buckbean
Buckwheat
Buckwheat (roasted) Kasha
Buckwheat whole grain
Bulgur (cereals)
Bush beans
Butter (half fat)
Butter beans white
Butter organic
Camembert
Campari
Capers in olive oil
Cardamom
Carob flour, St. john's bread

Carp
Carrot
Carrot (Early Carrot)
Carrot juice without sugar
Cashews
Cauliflower
Celery root
Celery sticks
Chamomile
Chamomile tea
Champignon
Channa-Dal
Chanterelle
Chard
Cherry (sour)
Cherry compote
Chervil
Chervil dried
Chestnut puree
Chicken Blood
Chicken egg white
Chicken heart
Chicken liver
Chicken meat
Chicken stomach
Chickweed
Chicory
Chinese cabbage
Chinese pearl barley
Chocolate
Chocolate (Diabetic)
Chrysanthemum blossom tea
Clarified butter
Clementine
Coconut fat
Coconut flakes
Coconut grated
Coconut meat
Codfish
Cola drink
Cola drink (low calorie)
Compote (fruits of the season)
Cooking oil
Coriander
Coriander (fresh)
Corn
Corn (fast polenta)
Corn (roasted)
Corn flour
Corn germ oil
Corn Grease (Polenta)
Corn silk tea
Corn starch
Cottage cheese

Couscous
Cranberries
Cranberry
Cranberry jam
Cream (30% fat)
Cream 10% coffee cream
Cream sour 10%
Cream sour 20%
Cream sour 30%
Creamer
Cress
Crispbread
Crucian
Cucumber (bitter)
Cucumber (spicy cucumber)
Cumin (Caraway seed)
Curcuma
Currant jam (black)
Currant jam (red)
Currant juice (black)
Currants (black)
Currants (red)
Curry paste red
Daisy
Dandelion juice
Dashi
Dates red
Deer's Bones
Deer's kidneys
Dill
Ducks egg
Dulse (seaweed)
Dyer's broom herb
Edam cheese
Eel smoked
Elderberries
Emmental cheese
Evening primrose oil
Fennel seeds ground
Fenugreek (Trigonella foenum-graecum)
Fernet Branca (herbal bitter liqueur)
Feta cheese
Fig
Fig dried
Fish innards
Fish pieces mixed (fresh water)
Fish remains
Fish sauce
Flounder
Flower pollen
Fox nut, gorgon nut, makhana
Fresh cheese from soya
Fresh cheese with herbs

Freshwater crab
Freshwater fish
Fructose (glucose)
Fruit mix juice
Fruit tea
Gail plum
Galangal
Garam Masala powder
Gelatin white
Gelee Royal
Gentian root
Gentian root tea
Ginger oil
Ginkgo fruit
Ginseng
Ginseng liqueur
Ginseng root
Goat and sheep's blood
Goat and sheep's brain
Goat and sheep's liver
Goat and sheep's milk
Goat and sheep's stomach
Goat cheese
Goose blood
Goose fat
Gorgonzola
Gouda cheese
Gourd
Grape juice red
Grape juice white
Grapefruit (Pomelo)
Grapefruit dried peel
Grapefruit juice
Grapes red
Grapeseed oil
Greengage
Ground
Ground caraway
Guava
Halibut (Flatfish)
Hazelnuts
Herbal tea mix
Herbs bitter
Herbs of Provence
Herbs various
Herbs wild
Herring
Hibiscus
Hibiscus tea
Hijiki
Hokkaido pumpkin
Honey wine (Met)
Hop
Horehound leaves

Horse meat
Iceberg lettuce
Jasmine blossoms tee
Jellyfish
Kaki plum
Kalmus
Kidney beans (red)
King Solomon's-seal
Kudzu
Kukicha tea
Ladyfingers
Lamb kidneys
Lamb liver
Lamb's lettuce
Lavender blossoms
Leaf salads (bitter)
Lemon Balm (dried)
Lemon Balm (fresh)
Lemongrass
Lentils black
Lentils red
Licorice root tea
Lily bulbs
Lima beans
Lime blossom tea
Linseed
Linseed (crushed)
Linseed oil
Liver smoothing tea
Loquate / Japanese medlar
Lotus roots
Lotus seeds
Lovage
Lovage seeds
Luo Han Guo fruit
Lychee liqueur
Lye roll
Mackerel
Malt
Mango juice
Manioc flour
Maple syrup
Mare's milk
Marjoram
Martini
Mascarpone cheese
Mayonnaise 50%
Mayonnaise 80%
Mediterranean fish (cod, plaice,
haddock, sea eel, mackerel)
Medlar
Millet
Millet flakes
Mineral water

Mirabelle plum
Miso
Miso black (fermented)
Mixed Pickles
Morel (black, dried)
Morel, dried
Mu Erh Mushroom
Muesli
Mulled Wine Spice
Mullet
Multi-grain bread (gray bread)
Mung bean sprouting
Mustard
Mustard Dijon
Mustard medium hot
Mustard sweet
Nasturtium (nose-twister or nose-tweaker)
Nectarine
Nettles
Noodles (wheat) with egg
Noodles (wheat, lasagne) with egg
Noodles (wheat, ribbon noodles) with egg
Noodles (wheat, spaghetti) with egg
Noodles (whole grain) with egg
Nori, purple seaweed, red algae
Octopus
Octopus
Olive oil
Olives green
Orange blossom
Orange dried peel
Orange grated peel
Orange jam
Orange peel
Oregano fresh
Oyster shell powder
Palm oil
Parsley root
Passion blossoms tea
Passion fruit
Peanut (roasted)
Peanut butter
Peanut oil
Peanuts
Pearl barley
Pearl barley
Peas, green
Pepper (ground)
Pepper powder (hot)
Pepper white (ground)
Peppermint
Peppermint tea

Pepperoni
Pepperoni, red, pitted, halved
Pepperoni, yellow, pitted, halved
Peppers (sweet)
Peppers powder
Pickle
Pig blood
Pigeon egg
Pine nuts
Pinto beans speckled
Pistachios
Plum dried
Plums
Pork Bacon
Pork brain
Pork fat (lard)
Pork ham
Pork ham cooked
Pork ham smoked
Pork heart
Pork kidneys
Pork knuckle
Pork Lard
Pork lung
Pork marrow bones
Pork sausage (Bratwurst) Pork skin
Pork/beef sausage (smoked)
Pork's intestine
Potato (mealy)
Potato flour
Prickly pear
Processed cheese 12%
processed cheese 30%
Prosecco
Psyllium seed
Pudding powder vanilla
Puff pastry
Pumpernickel (dark bread)
Pumpkin seeds
Quail egg
Rabbit
Rabbit (wild)
Rabbit liver
Rabbit meat
Radicchio
Radish horseradish
Radish leaves
Rapeseed oil
Raspberry jam
Raspberry leaf tea
Red beet
Red berry (without sugar)
Red cabbage
Reishi mushroom

Ribworttea
Rice (Gaoliang / Sorghum)
Rice (whole grain)
Rice flour
Rice long grain rice
Rice mash
Rice round grain
Rice starch
Rice sticky
Rice variety any
Rose blossom tea
Rose hip
Rose leaf tea
Rosefish
Rum
Rusk
Rye wholemeal bread
Safflower (Dyer's thistle / Hong Hua)
Saffron
Salmon
Salsify
Salt
Salt (herbal)
Savory
Savoy cabbage / kale
Sea buckthorn
Sea cucumber
Sesame oil
Sesame oil roasted
Sesame paste (Tahini)
Sesame, black
Sesame, white
Sheep's milk
Sheep's milk yoghurt
Sherry (whine)
Shiitake, dried
Shrimps
Skim milk powder
Slug
Sourdough
Soy flour
Soy noodles
Soy Tofu
Soy Tofu smoked
Soya Cuisine (soy cream)
Soybean milk
Soybeans
Soybeans, black
Soybeans, blacks, fermented
Spelled flakes
Spurdog (spiny dogfish, Schillerlocken)
St. Benedict's thistle, blessed thistle,
holy thistle, spotted thistle
Stevia (candyleaf, sweetleaf)

Strawberry jam
Sugar - icing sugar
Sugar molasses
Sugar palm sugar
Sugar substitute (sweetener)
Sunflower seeds
Supplementary nutrition
Sweet potato
Tabasco
Tarragon (Estragon)
Tea mixture uric acid lowering
Thistle oil
Thyme dried
Toast bread (whole grain)
Tomato dried
Tomato juice
Tomato paste
Tomato puree
Tonic Water
Topinambur
Trout
Trout (smoked)
Truffle
Tsampa (roasted barley flour)
Turkey breast meat
Turkey ham
Turmeric (yellow root)
Turnip
Turnips
Umeboshi paste
Valerian
Vanilla
Vanilla pod
Vanilla powder
Vanilla sugar natural
Vegetable juice
Vinegar (Red wine vinegar)
Vinegar Aceto Balsamico
Vinegar Aceto Balsamico white
Wakame
Walnut oil
Walnuts roasted
Wax gourd
Wheat flatbread/pita bread
Wheat flour whole grain
Wheat germ oil
Wheat/Rye/Gray-black bread with yeast
Wheatgrass juice
Wheatgrass powder
Whey
White beans
White bread (baguette)
White bread (pretzel sticks)
White bread (roll)

White bread (wheat bread)
White breadcrumbs
White cabbage
White dumpling bread (wheat bread cut into chunks)
Whitefish
Whole grain bread
Wholemeal flour
Wild garlic (garlic spinach)
Wild herbs

Wild strawberries
Wormwood
Wormwood herb
Yam root, yam root tuber
Yarrow
Yeast
Yew nut
Yoghurt vanilla
Zucchini

10.2 Use ingredients: yes

Almond marzipan
Almond milk
Almond puree
Apricot
Apricots
Basic recipe for a rice soup (Congee)
Beef fillet
Beef meat
Beef meatbones
Beef stomach
Black tea
Calamari
Chenpi (chinese tangerine bowl)
Chestnuts
Chickpeas
Chlorella (fresh water)
Coconut milk
Cod
Coix (seeds) YiYi Ren
Dates dried
Deer meat
Eel
Elderberry blossom tee
Endive salad
French beans
Goose
Goose egg
Goose parts
Grass carp
Green tea
Kombu seaweed (Saccharina japonica)
Kumquats
Lemon peel
Lettuce
Lobster
Longane
Margarine
Margarine (diet)
Mung bean
Okra
Olives

Oyster mushroom
Oysters
Papaya
Parsnip
Peas
Peppers
Perch
Pigeon
Plaice
Pork stomach
Potato
Pumpkin
Pumpkin seed oil
Quail
Quince
Quinoa
Radish
Radish black
Raisins
Rice (fragrance)
Rice Basmati
Rice black
Rice noodles
Rice red
Rice sweet
Rice wild (nature rice)
Romaine lettuce / lettuce salad
Rye
Rye flour
Sage
Sago (cereals)
Shark
Shrimp
Soybean oil
Soybeans, yellow
Spiny lobsters
Sugar brown
Sunflower oil
Tuna
Walnuts
Water

Water hot
Wheat
Wheat bulgur
Wheat flakes

Wheat flour
Wheat semolina
Wheat semolina for children

10.3 Use ingredients: little

Anchovy / Sardine
Anise (Common Fennel)
Bean oil
Blackberry's
Black-eyed peas
Blueberry
Blueberry juice
Boxhorn clover seeds
Buttermilk
Cereal coffee
Cherry
Cherry juice
Chicken egg
Chicken yolk
Chives
Clementines
Clove
Cocoa
Coffee
Cranberry
Cranberry juice
Cream, sweet 30%
Créme fraiche cheese
Curd cheese 20%
Curd cheese 40%
Currant (black)
Currant (red)
Currant (white)
Deer meat
Duck (heart)
Duck (slaughtered)
Fennel
Fennel tea
Feta cheese
Fresh cheese
Ginger fresh
Gooseberry
Grapes white
Green spelt
Hawthorn
Hyssop
Juniper berry
Kefir
Kohlrabi
Leek
Lentils

Lentils yellow
Lychee
Lychee in Preserved
Mallow (Malva sylvestris) blossom tea
Mustard seeds
Oat
Oat flakes (whole grain)
Oat flakes roasted
Oat flour
Oat fusion (baby food)
Oat meal
Oat milk
Onion (shallot)
Onion (spring onion)
Onion read
Onion white
Oregano dried
Parsley
Peaches
Peaches (canned)
Pear
Pear juice
Pepper Cayenne
Peppercorns
Peppers (rose peppers)
Pheasant
Pineapple
Pineapple (from a can)
Pineapple juice without sugar
Pomegranate
Poppy
Pork liver
Raspberry
Raspberry dried (immature)
Red wine
Rice malt
Rose hip tea
Rosemary
Sake
Sauerkraut (cutted cabbage fermented)
Sour cherries
Sour cream 15% fat
Sour milk
Sour milk cheese 20%
Spelled (Dark) bread
Spelled grain

Spelled semolina
Spelled wholemeal flour
Star anise
Strawberries
Strawberry Juice

Tangerine
Thyme
Umeboshi plums (Japanese apricots)
Vinegar (Apple vinegar)
White wine

10.4 Do not use contra-acting foods

Agar agar (kelp)
Amaranth
Apple (sour)
Asparagus (green or white)
Aubergine
Avocado
Banana
Banana (cooking banana)
Beer (Pils)
Beer (Top-fermented German dark beer)
Burdock root tea
Cantaloupe
Carambola (Star fruit)
Caviar
Chili (pod or ground)
Cinnamon ground
Cinnamon sticks
Cow's milk (1.5% fat)
Cow's milk (whole milk 3.5% fat)
Crab
Cucumber
Curry
Dandelion (young plants)
Dandelionroots tea
Garlic
Ginger powder
Goat
Honey
Kiwi
Lamb bones
Lamb meat
Lamb shoulder
Lamb's lettuce
Lemon
Lemon juice
Lime
Mango

Miso paste (soy bean paste)
Mold cheese
Mozzarella
Mulberry fruit
Mussels
Mutton
Mutton
Nutmeg
Orange
Orange juice
Parmesan
Pimento
Plum
Pork meat
Radish (white, green, purple-red)
Rhubarb
Rucola
Seacrab
Sorrel
Soy sauce
Spinach
Spirit
Sugar candy white
Sugar cane sugar
Sugar fructose - fruit sugar
Sugar glucose - grapes sugar
Sugar Milk Sugar
Sugar white
Tomato
Watermelon
Wheat beer
Wheat bran
Wild boar meat
Yarrow tea
Yogi tea
Yogurt (natural, 1.5% fat)
Yogurt (natural, 3.5% fat)

11 Herbs and their effects

11.1 Lady's mantle

thermal effect: neutral
taste: bitter
Do not use during pregnancy. Emanates moisture, tones qi, regulates
and moves qi, deters, quenches and regulates bleeding.
Due to its high tannin content and its astringent effect, the Lady's mantle
has anti-inflammatory and healing properties. In diarrhea no sugar should
be used in tea.

11.2 Coriander

thermal effect: warm
taste: spicy
Driving sweat, reducing wind, draining moisture, tonifying and regulating
qi, eliminating wind-cold.
The essential oils are appetizing, digestive, cramping and soothing in
stomach and intestinal disorders.

11.3 Herbs various

Stimulates appetite. Effect different.
Appetizing, lots of trace elements and vitamins.

11.4 Cress

thermal effect: cool
taste: sweet
Moves and tonifies qi and blood, diuretic, cools in internal heat,
moisturizes lungs, triggers stagnation, heads upwards.
Diuretic, supports urination. Good to fight dry mouth, inner agitation, sore
throat, diabetes, kidney stones, gastrointestinal complaints, lung
problems, menstrual cramps or cancer.

11.5 Lovage

thermal effect: warm
taste: spicy, bitter
Reduces inner wind and moisture, dissolves stagnation, directs upward,
warms Yang, regulates and moves Qi, warms inside, dissolves mucus-
cold, eliminates wind-cold.
Stimulates digestion, reduces pain. Extracts of the root are used to flush
out urinary tract infections and prevent kidney gravel.

11.6 Lily bulbs

thermal effect: cool
taste: sweet, bitter
Tonifies Yin, soothes Shen / Spirit. Moisturizes the lungs, clears heat and
stops coughing.
Calms nerves, good to fight scaly skin. The onions and the petals are
added to ointments in the Orient, which can heal muscles and tendons.
White lily (astringent).

11.7 Marjoram

thermal effect: warm
taste: spicy
Dissolves stagnation, heads upwards. Regulates and moves Qi,
eliminates wind-cold, dissolves slime-cold, calms down Shen / Spirit,
suppresses inner wind, moves blood.
Helps to digest fat foods, strengthens digestive organs, helps to fight
colds, strengthens menstruation, promotes skin healing.

11.8 Balm

thermal effect: warm
taste: bitter
Keep the fluids, pulls together, soothe lever fire, soothe Shen, stimulate
Lung Qi. Regulates qi, eliminates heat caused by yin deficiency.
Soothing effect, Good for insomnia, restlessness and upset stomach,
Allergies, Asthma, Migraine, Flatulence, Headache, Rheumatism and
mental tension. To strengthen after cold and infectious diseases.

11.9 Parsley

thermal effect: warm
taste: bitter
Nourishes blood and liver, harmonizes liver and spleen, strengthens eyesight, preserves juices, contracts. Dissolves moisture and warms Yang.
Stimulates liver function, detoxifies. Forces urinating. Relieves flatulence. Digestive and menstrual stimulating, birth-accelerating, memory-enhancing, blood-purifying, skin-smoothing.

11.10   Rosemary

thermal effect: warm
taste: bitter
Dries out, leads down. Strengthens the heart, lungs and spleen qi, strengthens liver blood. Strengthens heart-Yin. Expels spleen heat / cold moisture. Strengthens spleen and kidney yang.
Promotes digestion, relieves bloating, strengthens lung, spleen and kidney. Affects the circulation and nerves. Appetizing. Baths help to fight circulatory disorders as well as with gout and rheumatism.

11.11   Sage

thermal effect: neutral
taste: bitter, spicy
Expels slime, guides down, strengthens Qi, eliminates Wind-Heat, eliminate heat induced by Yin deficiency.
Good to fight yeast infections. The leaves have a digestive effect and are used in greasy foods. Antiperspirant effect. Helps to relieve coughing attacks. Dries out.

11.12   King Solomon's-seal

thermal effect: neutral
taste: sweet, bitter
Tonifies Yin and Qi, astringent, tonifies blood, eliminates wind-cold / heat-wetness.
Used to repair wounds or damaged tissue. Good to fight dry cough, earlier also tuberculosis and dysentery, as well as diarrhea and hemorrhoids.

11.13 Yam root, yam root tuber

thermal effect: neutral
taste: sweet
Tonifies Yin, Yang and Qi, reduces inner wind, dissolves wetness, warms Yang.
Solves cramps (in the gastrointestinal tract). Digestive through increased bile production. Anti-inflammatory in rheumatic diseases.
Mucolytic agent for coughing. Relief of menopausal symptoms.

11.14 Lemon Balm (fresh)

thermal effect: cool
taste: sour
Soothes Shen / Spirit, regulates and moves Qi, eliminates heat caused by Yin deficiency, tones Qi.
Stimulating, antibacterial, encouraging, relaxing, antispasmodic, cooling, antipyretic, analgesic, sweat-inducing, virus-
inhibiting. Good for colds, fever, flu, cough, bronchitis, asthma, loss of appetite, bloating, heartburn.

12 Basics of Nutrition

The basic principles of nutrition described herein are general recommendations. They are not aimed at a specific form of therapy. Recommendations concerning a therapy have priority.

12.1 Nutrition

Regular meals in a relaxed atmosphere. A warm breakfast is considered a good start into the day.

The main meals ought to be taken for lunch – supper in the early evening. Pay attention to feeling hungry or sated: don't eat too much nor remain hungry is the rule

Prepare the meals freshly from natural, regional products. Frozen, heat-conserved, industrially prepared or foodstuffs cooked in the microwave oven are rejected.

Choice of foodstuffs according to the season: more cooling food in summer, more warming food in winter.

Eat cooked food at least twice a day. Food and drinks ought to be lukewarm, never ice-cold or hot.

Raw vegetables, briefly cooked vegetables, freshly squeezed juices and mineral water are not recommended. Milk and dairy products are only included in the diet if they don't cause problems. Don't use therapeutic recipes over a longer period without consulting your doctor or therapist.

Varied food
Enjoy the diversity of foodstuffs. Characteristics of a balanced nutrition are variety, suitable combination and a balanced quantity of rich and low energy foodstuffs (on one hand avoiding undersupply with essential nutrients and on the other hand to take to many undesirable substances).

A lot of Cereal Products - and Potatoes
Bread, pasta, rice, cereal flakes (best wholemeal) as well as potatoes contain almost no fat, but many vitamins, mineral nutrients, trace elements, roughage and secondary plant substances. These foodstuffs ought to be taken with low-fat side dishes.

Vegetables and Fruit – „Take Five" every day ... 5 portions of vegetables and fruit a day, as fresh as possible, briefly cooked, or maybe one portion as a juice – ideal as a side dish to every meal as well as snack between meals: Thus a lot of vitamins, mineral nutrients as well as roughage and secondary plant substances

Daily milk and dairy products

Milk and Dairy Products every Day, once or twice per Week Fish; meat, sausages as well as eggs moderately. These foodstuffs contain valuable nutrients like calcium in the milk, iodine selenium and omega-3 fat acids in saltwater fish. Meat is favorable due to its high content of disposable iron and the vitamins B1, B6 and B12. Quantities of 300 – 600 g meat and sausage per week are sufficient. Prefer low-fat products, especially in meat- and dairy products.

Low-fat and fatty Foodstuffs
Fat supplies us with essential fat acids and fatty foodstuffs contain also fat-soluble vitamins. Fat is high in energy; therefore much fat in the food may cause overweight, possibly also cancer. Too many saturated fat acids may further a tendency for cardio-vascular diseases in the long term. Prefer vegetable oils and fats (e.g. rapeseed-, olive-, soya-oils and solid fats produced therefrom). Beware of invisible fat in meat- and dairy products, pastry and sweets as well as in fast-food and convenience foods. 70 – 90 g fat per day is sufficient.

Moderately Sugar and Salt
Take sugar and foods/drinks containing various kinds of sugar (e.g. glucose syrup) only occasionally. Use herbs and spices as well as a little salt creatively. Prefer salt containing iodine.

Plenty of Liquids
Water is absolutely essential. Drink 1-2 l liquids every day. Prefer water (with or without gas) and other low-calorie drinks. Alcoholic drinks should not be taken.

Tasty Dishes, carefully cooked
Cook the meals with as low temperatures and as short as possible, using little water and fat – this preserves the original taste, keeps the nutrients intact and prevents the production of harmful compounds.

Take time and enjoy the food
Take your Time and enjoy your Food
Eating consciously helps to eat right. The eye enjoys food, too. It's fun, invites to enjoy varied dishes and stimulates the feeling of satiety.

Watch your Weight and stay in Motion
A balanced diet and a lot of exercise and sport (30 – 60 min/day) are a healthy combination. The right weight furthers well-being and health.
Thermals, directional effectiveness, digestive power
There are various criteria for judging the effectiveness of herbs and

foodstuffs.

The use of certain herbs and ingredients is based on observations of the effects on the body which these foodstuffs, herbs and spices show after having eaten them. The medical science has developed following system: Every ingredient or herb has a directional effectiveness. Furthermore, there are herbs which have a special effect on certain organs.

The basic condition for a healthy metabolism is to obtain sufficient energy from food and that the digestive process doesn't use too much energy. An easily digestible meal makes content and sated, doesn't cause flatulence and fatigue after the meal. The perfect spices increase the healthiness of our meals. Very often, just small doses of herbs and spices will suffice. They are not used to make us sated, but to help our digestive organs to digest the food.

12.2 Recipes

The recipes list the ingredients to be used and the cooking instructions show how the dish is prepared. The list of ingredients shows the concerned quantities as well as the relevance for the therapy. If you find „less than mentioned", try to comply or find an alternative from the „list of recommended foodstuffs". Mostly it shall result just in a small change of taste when you simply avoid this ingredient.

Mild cooking methods: boiling, stewing, poaching, steaming
Strong cooking methods: barbecuing, roasting, frying, smoking
Balanced cooking methods: deep-frying, baking brick
Deep-freezing and warming in the microwave oven should be avoided (denaturalization).

12.3 Foodstuffs

Foodstuffs have an effect on body and soul like medicinal herbs, only a very much milder one. Dietary advice is mainly based on regional foodstuffs. The knowledge about the effects of each foodstuff and the knowledge, when which foodstuff shall be used, is based on the orthodox school of medicine. Use ecologic-organic products, if possible. As everything should be cooked for a long time due to a better digestability and very rarely eaten raw, the food agrees with everyone.

The classification of the foodstuffs according to their effect on the body is the basis in order to achieve a harmonious status of health.

Dietary advisors do not recommend certain foodstuffs for everyone. The individual diet is tailor-made for the individual constitution.

Buy only fresh and ripe fruit and vegetables. You ought to leave unripe fruit and vegetables and such with brown spots and wilted leaves behind in the market. In this case take deep-frozen goods (never ready-to-serve dishes!). Fruit and vegetables are deep-frozen immediately after harvesting and often contain more vitamins and minerals than the goods from the vegetable shelf. Whereas conserved or tinned goods contain very much less biological substances. Also, salt, sugar and others are mostly added to the latter. Never leave the foodstuffs in the water after washing them to avoid that many vital substances get drowned. Clean salads, fruit and vegetables immediately before serving.

Please make sure of the hygienic processing of foodstuffs. Clean your salads, fruit and vegetables carefully. When cooking with meat, prepare all ingredients first and then process the meat products. Clean the worktop and tools very carefully. Wooden surfaces ought to be treated with a mild disinfectant regularly in order to reduce germination. Store fruit and vegetables separately, if possible. Harvested fruit and vegetables are still alive and emit e.g. ethylene gas, which makes other products ripen and age faster. Keep meat and fish in the closed packaging or store them in the fridge in closed containers.

12.4 Herbs

There are some basic rules for storing medicinal herbs. On principle, herbs must be protected from direct sunlight, humidity and heat.

Containers for the storage of herbs may be glasses, ceramic jars and even plastic containers. However, plastic is a rather unsuitable material and should only be a short-term solution. In case of glass containers, use a dark material.

Medicinal herbs cannot be kept for any long period. The shelf life of herbs is limited. However, it can be prolonged with suitable storage. The place should be dark, rather cool and absolutely dry. A wooden medicine cabinet, placed not directly next to a source of heat, would be ideal. Never buy large quantities of herbs so as not to have to throw them away. Label the container with the name of the herb and the date of harvesting or processing.

13 Other dietic-books

The following syndromes of dietetics, TCM or for a therapy supplement for cancer are available.

Dietetics

E001. Nutrition of the infant - baby food
E002. Nutrition during lactation
E003. Nutrition in old age
E004. Nutrition of children and adolescents
E005. Nutrition of athletes
E006. Light weight
E007. Pregnancy
E008. Full food

Protein and electrolyte - kidneys
E009. (hemodialysis) dialysis treatment
E010. Acute renal failure
E011. Chronic renal insufficiency
E012. Nephrotic syndrome
E013. Kidney stones (nephrolithiasis)

Gastrointestinal tract - pancreas
E014. Acute pancreatitis (inflammation of the pancreas)
E015. Chronic pancreatitis (inflammation of the pancreas)

Gastrointestinal tract - small intestine and large intestine
E016. Acute obstipation (constipation)
E017. Chronic obstipation (constipation)
E018. Colon irritabile
E019. Diverticulitis
E020. Acquired lactose intolerance (lactose malabsorption)
E021. Fructose malabsorption
E022. Glutensensitive enteropathy (celiac disease)
E023. Colectomy
E024. Short Bowel Syndrome

Gastrointestinal tract - liver, gallbladder, bile ducts
E025. Acute and chronic hepatitis (inflammation of the liver)
E026. Cholelithiasis (bile stones)
E027. fatty liver
E028. cirrhosis

Gastrointestinal tract - Stomach and duodenal intestine
E029. Acute gastritis
E030. Chronic gastritis
E031. Stomach bleeding
E032. Ulcus ventriculi and duodenal ulcer
E033. Condition after gastric surgery

Gastrointestinal tract - oral cavity and esophagus

E034. Stomatitis
E035. Esophageal carcinoma (esophageal cancer)
E036. Refluosophagitis (heartburn)

Special diseases
E037. Phenylketonuria (PKU)
E038. Rheumatic joint diseases

E039. **Metabolism** Obesity (overweight)
E040. Diabetes mellitus
E041. Eating disorders (underweight)

Fat metabolism
E042. Hypercholesterolaemia (increased cholesterol level)
E043. Hepatic Encephalopathy

Heart and circulation
E044. Arteriosclerosis (arterial calcification)
E045. Heart insufficiency
E046. Hypertension
E047. Hyperuricaemia and gout

E048. **Changed nutrient requirements** In case of fever
E049. For malignant diseases
E050. After burns
E051. Radiation and chemotherapy

E100. **CANCER** Pancreatic cancer
E101. Bladder cancer
E102. Blood cancer (leukemia)
E103. Breast cancer
E104. Colorectal cancer
E105. Gastric cancer
E106. Kidney cancer
E107. Esophageal cancer

E200. **TCM** Bladder - moisture heat in the bladder Bladder - moisture and cold in the bladder
        Bladder - emptiness and cold in the bladder
E201. Large intestine - external cold affects the large intestine Large intestine - moisture heat
        in the large intestine
E202. Large intestine - heat blocks the intestine II acute
E203. Large intestine - dryness of the colon
E204. Large intestine - Yang deficiency (cold)
E205. Heart - Blood insufficiency
E206. Heart - Blood stagnation
E207. Heart - Fire
E208. Heart - Hot mucus clogs the heart pores
E209. Heart - Cold mucus clogs the heart pores
E210. Heart - Qi deficiency
E211. Heart - Yang deficiency
E212. Heart - Yin deficiency
E213. Liver - Ascending Liver Yang
E214. Liver - Blood deficiency
E215. Liver - Blood stagnation

E216. Liver - Moisture heat in liver and gall bladder Liver - Fire
E217. Liver - Gall bladder Qi-Empty Liver - Cold in the liver meridian
E218. Liver - Qi stagnation Liver - Wind Liver - Wind with ascending liver Yang
E219. Liver - Wind with blood anemic
E220. Liver - Wind with extreme heat
E221. Lung - Qi deficiency Lung - Mucus-moisture in the lungs
E222. Lung - Mucus-heat in the lungs
E223. Lung - Mucus-cold in the lungs
E224. Lung - Dryness of the lungs
E225. Lung - Wind-heat attacks the lungs
E226. Lung - Wind-cold affects the lungs
E227. Lung - Yin deficiency
E228. Stomach - Bloodstagnation Stomach - Fire
E229. Stomach - Cold with liquid
E230. Stomach - Nutrition stagnation
E231. Stomach - Qi deficiency
E232. Stomach - Rebellious Qi
E233. Stomach - Yin Emptiness
E234. Spleen - Heat and moisture attack the spleen
E235. Spleen - Coldness and moisture affects the spleen
E236. Spleen - Qi deficiency
E237. Spleen - Qi deficiency + Declining spleen Qi
E238. Spleen - Qi deficiency + spleen does not control the blood
E239. Spleen - Yang deficiency
E240. Kidney - Heart and kidney no longer communicate
E241. Kidney - Jing deficiency
E242. Kidney - Kidneys cannot receive the Qi
E243. Kidney - Qi is not stable
E244. Kidney - Yang deficiency
E245. Kidney - Yin deficiency

For further information visit di-book.com.